AF443652

GHOST WORLD

BY JAMES McLURE

★

DRAMATISTS
PLAY SERVICE
INC.

Copyright ©, 1995, by James McLure

CAUTION: Professionals and amateurs are hereby warned that GHOST WORLD is subject to a royalty. It is fully protected under the copyright laws of the United States of America, and of all countries covered by the International Copyright Union (including the Dominion of Canada and the rest of the British Commonwealth), and of all countries covered by the Pan-American Copyright Convention and the Universal Copyright Convention, and of all countries with which the United States has reciprocal copyright relations. All rights, including professional, amateur, motion picture, recitation, lecturing, public reading, radio broadcasting, television, video or sound taping, all other forms of mechanical or electronic reproduction, such as information storage and retrieval systems and photocopying, and the rights of translation into foreign languages, are strictly reserved. Particular emphasis is laid upon the question of readings, permission for which must be secured from the Author's agent in writing.

The stage performance rights in GHOST WORLD (other than first class rights) are controlled exclusively by the DRAMATISTS PLAY SERVICE, INC., 440 Park Avenue South, New York, N.Y. 10016. No professional or non-professional performance of the play (excluding first class professional performance) may be given without obtaining in advance the written permission of the DRAMA-TISTS PLAY SERVICE, INC., and paying the requisite fee.

Inquiries concerning all other rights should be addressed to Mary Harden, c/o Bret Adams, Ltd., 448 West 44th Street, New York, N.Y. 10036.

SPECIAL NOTE

All groups receiving permission to produce GHOST WORLD are required to give credit to the Author as sole and exclusive Author of the Play in all programs distributed in connection with performances of the Play and in all instances in which the title of the Play appears for purposes of advertising, publicizing or otherwise exploiting the Play and/or a production thereof; the name of the Author must appear on a separate line, in which no other name appears, immediately beneath the title and in size of type equal to 50% of the largest letter used for the title of the Play. No person, firm or entity may receive credit larger or more prominent than that accorded the Author.

SPECIAL NOTE ON SONGS AND RECORDINGS

For performance of such songs, arrangements and recordings mentioned in this play as are protected by copyright, the permission of the copyright owners must be obtained; or other songs and recordings in the public domain substituted.

GHOST WORLD was produced by Theatre/Theatre (Jeff Murray, Artistic Director), in Los Angeles, California, on February 25, 1994. It was directed by Jeff Murray; the set design was by Evan Bartoletti; the lighting and sound designs were by Person Impersonator and the stage manager was Henry Harris. The cast was as follows:

PENDERTON .... Will Utay
JACKIE JACK............................... Ritchie Marron Montgomery

GHOST WORLD was produced by the West Bank Downstairs Theatre (Rand Forrester, Artistic Director; Patricia Miller, Managing Director), in New York City, in December, 1993, under the the title THE COINCIDENCE. It was directed by Richard Harden and the stage manager was Lee O'Conner. The cast was as follows:

PENDERTON .... Tim Wahrer
JACKIE .... Dennis Predovic

CHARACTERS

PENDERTON: A staid, proper, gentlemen. Conservative. Intellectual. Wears suspenders and a belt. He wears a three piece suit and a Mets' cap.

JACKIE JACK, THE STURGEON KING: A wild March hare. Wears a loud Hawaiian shirt, sunglasses, a straw hat, loose khaki pants, and smokes an unlit cigar about the size of his leg. He's dressed rather shabbily.

SETTING

A park. Spring. A park bench.

GHOST WORLD

Penderton sitting on the bench reading The New York Times. *Sighs. Enjoying the day. Jackie Jack enters carrying a bag. He goes to the trash bin. Finds a small half-pint of Whiskey with a swallow left. He drinks it. He goes to the bench, sits.*

JACKIE JACK.   What a coincidence ... (*He takes a napkin out of his bag, spreads it on his lap. He takes a half-eaten sandwich out of his hat and begins to eat.*) What a coincidence. I say.... What a coincidence.

PENDERTON.   I beg your pardon?

JACKIE JACK.   What a coincidence. You're a Mets fan — I'm a Mets fan — what a coincidence.

PENDERTON.   Uh, yes.

JACKIE JACK.   It was the cap that tipped me off.

PENDERTON.   Wow.

JACKIE JACK.   Dead giveaway.

PENDERTON.   As a matter of fact, I'm also a Yankee fan.

JACKIE JACK.   What a coincidence. So am I.

PENDERTON.   I reject the parochialism of inner city rivalries.

JACKIE JACK.   What a coincidence. So do I.

PENDERTON.   I also like the Dodgers.

JACKIE JACK.   What a coincidence ... so do I.

PENDERTON.   (*Pompously.*) I like any team that plays competitive baseball.

JACKIE JACK.   Oh, I agree. (*Pause. Jackie finishes his sandwich. Folds the paper napkin into a flower and places the flower into his hat-band.*) Of course, my first love is the arts.

PENDERTON.   (*Skeptically.*) The arts.

JACKIE JACK.   Oh, yeah, sure. I love the theatre.

PENDERTON.   Oh, the theatre.

JACKIE JACK.   But I tell you something, my friend, the great days of experimental theatre are over.
PENDERTON.   You don't say.
JACKIE JACK.   Oh, yeah. I think it was Oscar Wilde that said it — "The more the avant-garde changes, the more it stays the same."
PENDERTON.   Oscar Wilde never said that —
JACKIE JACK.   What I'm trying to say here, pal, is where are the great experimental artists of today? Where's today's Joe Gherkin?
PENDERTON.   You mean Joe Chaikin.
JACKIE JACK.   *(Fondly.)* Ah, the work he did down at La Bomba —
PENDERTON.   La Mama.
JACKIE JACK.   And the playwrights? Where's today's Sam Collie?
PENDERTON.   Shepard.
JACKIE JACK.   What?
PENDERTON.   Shepard, not Collie. Shepard.
JACKIE JACK.   Look, we're talking playwrights here, not dogs.
PENDERTON.   Oh really? Well, I happen to be a playwright.
JACKIE JACK.   *(Delighted.)* Oh yeah? Me too! *(Pause.)*
PENDERTON.   A *published* playwright.
JACKIE JACK.   Oh yeah? Me too!
PENDERTON.   Of course, I also direct.
JACKIE JACK.   Say! What a coincidence! Me too!
PENDERTON.   I used to be an actor. But I gave it up.
JACKIE JACK.   I know what you mean. I gave it up, too. To concentrate on my writing. Ah — the theatre.
PENDERTON.   I'm also a composer.
JACKIE JACK.   This is incredible! Me too!
PENDERTON.   What have you composed?
JACKIE JACK.   Oh, nothing much lately, I'm afraid.
PENDERTON.   *(Smugly.)* I see.
JACKIE JACK.   Unless, of course, you count a few chamber pieces that I did for Julliard last month. *(Pause.)*
PENDERTON.   Have you ever done film?
JACKIE JACK.   Film?... Well, no.

PENDERTON.   (*Triumphant.*) Ah, well.
JACKIE JACK.   I mean ... I've got one in the *can* but it hasn't been released yet.
PENDERTON.   Oh *really?*
JACKIE JACK.   Yeah. It's a really complicated deal. You wouldn't believe it.
PENDERTON.   (*Pause.*) Yeah. I'm going out to L.A. next week.
JACKIE JACK.   Oh yeah?
PENDERTON.   Film thing.
JACKIE JACK.   Hey, congratulations. Me too. (*Pause.*)
PENDERTON.   Yeah — talking with some people at Tri-Star.
JACKIE JACK.   Tri-Star? Did you say Tri-Star?
PENDERTON.   Tri-Star.
JACKIE JACK.   I can't believe this!
PENDERTON.   Oh? Is Tri-Star where your film is in the *can* but not *released?*
JACKIE JACK.   No, no, no. That's at Disney.
PENDERTON.   Oh, Disney.
JACKIE JACK.   Yeah. Those schmucks. At Tri-Star I've got a three picture deal.
PENDERTON.   Three picture deal.
JACKIE JACK.   Right. Say, who're you talking to at Tri-Star?
PENDERTON.   (*Proudly.*) Bob Shapiro.
JACKIE JACK.   God, no.
PENDERTON.   (*Smugly.*) Yes.
JACKIE JACK.   Why? Bob's on the way out.
PENDERTON.   What?
JACKIE JACK.   Didn't you know? Bob's going to be fired.
PENDERTON.   What?!
JACKIE JACK.   Look, I personally like Bob. He's a bright, intelligent guy, but his instincts about what people want to see just *suck.* Look, he can always go back to being an agent, right?
PENDERTON.   He used to handle Shawna Steele.
JACKIE JACK.   And look what he did for *her.* The only picture of Shawna's that really bombed, Bob *produced!* I hate to say it, but Bob really sucks.
PENDERTON.   What?!

JACKIE JACK.   He carries absolutely no clout. What you oughta be doing is taking a meeting with David Fielder.
PENDERTON.   David Fielder? You know David Fielder? The head of production? The boy genius?
JACKIE JACK.   (Fondly.) Yeah. He's sorta like a kid brother to me. He's the one who begged me to sign the three picture deal.
PENDERTON.   Begged you.
JACKIE JACK.   Finally, I gave in. Provided I had the option of directing the third picture, of course.
PENDERTON.   Oh, so you're not going to direct your first two films at Tri-Star?
JACKIE JACK.   No — I figure I'll learn my craft first. After all, I'm no Orson Welles ... yet.
PENDERTON.   (Sarcastic.) But I'll bet you didn't want to leave the theatre, did you?
JACKIE JACK.   See there. I knew you'd understand. We're so much alike.
PENDERTON.   We're nothing alike.
JACKIE JACK.   I knew you couldn't stand to leave the theatre, either.
PENDERTON.   (Protesting.) Well, I'm just going to Hollywood once.
JACKIE JACK.   Well, of course.
PENDERTON.   With my hit play I bought a new co-op.
JACKIE JACK.   I made the same damn mistake myself.
PENDERTON.   My accountant said I'd be a fool not to.
JACKIE JACK.   Mine too.
PENDERTON.   Now someone's got to pay for it.
JACKIE JACK.   That's why it was a mistake.
PENDERTON.   So I have to move to Hollywood for the money.
JACKIE JACK.   Me too.
PENDERTON.   And yet I have reservations —
JACKIE JACK.   God, I hate to leave the theatre.
PENDERTON.   God, so do I.
JACKIE JACK.   But ... what the hell. The theatre's dead, right?

PENDERTON. Right. Dead.
JACKIE JACK. In all my years in New York —
PENDERTON. I've never seen it this dead —
JACKIE JACK. How long have you been in the city?
PENDERTON. Too long.
JACKIE JACK. Me too.
PENDERTON. Boy, those were the days, weren't they?
JACKIE JACK. We did theatre on a shoe-string budget.
PENDERTON. We were lucky to have shoestrings in those days.
JACKIE JACK. And God, it was great.
PENDERTON. God, we had passion!
JACKIE JACK. Passion! That's it — passion! We had passion! Now, the kids today —
PENDERTON. Oh! The kids today! Don't talk to me about the kids today! What do they have?
JACKIE JACK. Well, I'll tell you damn straight what they *don't* have!
PENDERTON. What's that?
JACKIE JACK. Passion!
PENDERTON. Passion! That's it! I couldn't have said it better myself!
JACKIE JACK. You just did.
PENDERTON. I know I did.
JACKIE JACK. We also had dedication!
PENDERTON. Dedication!
JACKIE JACK. Dreams!
PENDERTON. Dreams!
JACKIE JACK. Great teachers!
PENDERTON. Great teachers!
JACKIE JACK. Face it, man. The theatre's dead.
PENDERTON. It's dead.
JACKIE JACK. And you know who killed it?
PENDERTON. Who?
JACKIE JACK. The critics.
PENDERTON. The critics.
JACKIE JACK. The *Times*.
PENDERTON. Inflation.

JACKIE JACK.   My landlord.
PENDERTON.   Ronald Reagan.
JACKIE JACK.   Television.
PENDERTON.   MTV.
JACKIE JACK.   Madonna.
PENDERTON.   Bush.
JACKIE JACK.   Say, are you a Democrat?
PENDERTON.   Yes.
JACKIE JACK.   So am I! What a coincidence!
PENDERTON.   That doesn't prove anything.
JACKIE JACK.   One more thing we've got in common.
PENDERTON.   We have nothing in common.
JACKIE JACK.   That accent! Where were you born?
PENDERTON.   Brooklyn.
JACKIE JACK.   So was I!
PENDERTON.   See! I was just testing you! I was really born in Canton, Ohio.
JACKIE JACK.   I was just being polite. So was I. Born in Canton, Ohio. Good ol' Canton.
PENDERTON.   You weren't born in Canton, Ohio.
JACKIE JACK.   241 West Decater Street.
PENDERTON.   You weren't born at 241 West Decater Street.
JACKIE JACK.   Of course I was.
PENDERTON.   No, your accent is Brooklyn.
JACKIE JACK.   I was born in Canton and moved to Brooklyn when I was six.
PENDERTON.   *(Distraught.)* So did I.
JACKIE JACK.   See, we have a tremendous amount in common.
PENDERTON.   How did you know about 241 West Decater Street?
JACKIE JACK.   Because that's where I was born.
PENDERTON.   *(Adamantly.)* No you *weren't! I* was! I was born there!
JACKIE JACK.   What an incredible coincidence!
PENDERTON.   It's not a coincidence! It *can't* be a coincidence!
JACKIE JACK.   You're right! It probably isn't a coincidence.

Nothing in this world is a coincidence. Our lives have meaning, damnit!

PENDERTON.   Not necessarily.

JACKIE JACK.   You're right. We're bereft of hope.

PENDERTON.   Nevertheless —

JACKIE JACK.   *(Elated.)* You're right! We must all look on the positive side!

PENDERTON.   But there *is* no positive side.

JACKIE JACK.   *(Depressed.)* Well, of course not. I was a fool to assume there was one. Pardon me for being a simpleton.

PENDERTON.   But you're not a simpleton.

JACKIE JACK.   I'm not?

PENDERTON.   You're probably just schizophrenic.

JACKIE JACK.   Sure! That's right! I'm just schizophrenic! Why didn't we think of that ourselves!

PENDERTON.   Ok. Let's just wait a minute.

JACKIE JACK.   A minute? I've got all the time in the world. I wonder what DiMaggio is doing?

PENDERTON.   Joe DiMaggio. Who are you?

JACKIE JACK.   Well, that's kinda personal, doncha think? I don't go into your personal life.

PENDERTON.   How do you know about 241 West Decater Street?

JACKIE JACK.   Well, that's where I was born.

PENDERTON.   No — *you* weren't born there. I was born there.

JACKIE JACK.   *(Indignant.)* So! You think you're the only person who can be born at 241 West Decater? Who are you? The only person in the universe? *(Pause.)*

PENDERTON.   That was my home.

JACKIE JACK.   Mine too.

PENDERTON.   No, it wasn't.

JACKIE JACK.   Look, maybe it *is* just a coincidence.

PENDERTON.   No — this is some sort of scam.

JACKIE JACK.   Maybe *you're* the one pulling the scam! But you don't hear me complaining because we have so much in common.

PENDERTON.   We have *nothing* in common.

JACKIE JACK.   I love you. Can I say that?
PENDERTON.   Well, no.
JACKIE JACK.   I have an overwhelming urge to buy you tulips. Is that sensitive of me, or what?
PENDERTON.   No, it's just plain ridiculous.
JACKIE JACK.   Just for that, you don't get the tulips.
PENDERTON.   I don't want the tulips.
JACKIE JACK.   I don't have to do this, you know.
PENDERTON.   Wait a minute — you remind me of someone.
JACKIE JACK.   Well, it's about time.
PENDERTON.   I've met you before.
JACKIE JACK.   In a manner of speaking.
PENDERTON.   Somewhere.
JACKIE JACK.   What kind of tulips do you like? *(Like a magician, Jack produces a bunch of tulips.)*
PENDERTON.   I don't want your tulips.
JACKIE JACK.   I've got to repay you somehow.
PENDERTON.   Repay me? For what?
JACKIE JACK.   *(Dropping to his knees, kissing Penderton's hand.)* After all you've done for me — and you ask what? Whatta guy!
PENDERTON.   What's going on here. *(To audience.)* I know this guy. He's just pretending to be an idiot.
JACKIE JACK.   I love it when you talk obscene.
PENDERTON.   I'm not talking obscene —
JACKIE JACK.   *(Singing.)*
      Obscene —
      I'm just trying to be seen —
      You don't really know what I mean —
      But life is so obscene —
PENDERTON.   *(To audience.)* This guy's cunning and he uses words well. He's a linguist.
JACKIE JACK.   That's why all the girls like me.
PENDERTON.   Why?
JACKIE JACK.   I'm cunninglinguist. Ha-ha-ha.
PENDERTON.   Wait a minute! Wait a minute! That joke! Cunninglinguist — that's my joke.

JACKIE JACK.   They're *all* your jokes.
PENDERTON.   Wait a minute! Wait a minute!
JACKIE JACK.   (*Checking his watch.*) At this rate the universe stops.
PENDERTON.   241 Decater Street. Tulips. Cunninglinguist. You're "Jackie Jack, the Sturgeon King."
JACKIE JACK.   Now we're in Double Jeopardy, where the scores can really change. Have a sturgeon? (*Jack produces a sturgeon from his bag, hands it to Penderton. Horrified, Penderton throws it away.*)
PENDERTON.   You're a character out of a play of mine — a play that I never finished. I wrote the first act but I never finished it.
JACKIE JACK.   You're telling Noah about the flood.
PENDERTON.   What are you doing out and about?
JACKIE JACK.   Well, you never finished me. Where the hell am I supposed to go?
PENDERTON.   (*Hiding him.*) Look, we can't be seen like this.
JACKIE JACK.   Wait a minute. Are you ashamed to be seen with me in public?
PENDERTON.   Of course not — it's not that —
JACKIE JACK.   What am I? Just a ship that passed in the night?
PENDERTON.   Please don't raise your voice.
JACKIE JACK.   What the hell am I? A weekend in Rio?
PENDERTON.   Listen — I have a reputation to protect.
JACKIE JACK.   That's fine for you to say. You have other characters — other plays —
PENDERTON.   Look, it didn't work out, OK?
JACKIE JACK.   It was just one of those things, right?
PENDERTON.   Right.
JACKIE JACK.   So you think you can just dump me like last week's dirty laundry?
PENDERTON.   C'mon, be a good kid. Disappear.
JACKIE JACK.   Disappear? Who am I? Casper the Ghost?
PENDERTON.   Look, I thought a play about a guy who ran a fish market and called himself the Sturgeon King was a

funny idea. It wasn't, so I gave up.
JACKIE JACK.   Well, what am I supposed to do? Here I am running around without a second act. Living in parks, begging for a living. People think I'm a bum!
PENDERTON.   *(Taking out his wallet.)* Look, do you need any money?
JACKIE JACK.   Hey! What d'you think I am? Some kinda whore? How much money you got?
PENDERTON.   Oh, forty dollars.
JACKIE JACK.   *(Taking the money.)* Ok. If it'll soothe your social conscience.
PENDERTON.   Now — if you'd just go away.
JACKIE JACK.   Wham, bam, thank you Ma'am. Is that it?
PENDERTON.   Now, don't take it like that.
JACKIE JACK.   How am I supposed to take it?
PENDERTON.   We had a few laughs.
JACKIE JACK.   We did?
PENDERTON.   Not many. Otherwise, I'd have finished the second act.
JACKIE JACK.   So what happens now? I get shoved back in the drawer?
PENDERTON.   That's about it.
JACKIE JACK.   No! No! It's not that easy!
PENDERTON.   Listen, we meant something to each other at one point in time but it didn't work out. We gotta get on with our lives.
JACKIE JACK.   *You've* gotta get on with your life. Me? I don't even have a second act!
PENDERTON.   Listen to me, OK? An error in judgement — *(Penderton suddenly sees some people he recognizes. He waves to them. Affably.)* Hi there! Yes! Yes! I don't know him — I've never seen him before in my life! Goodbye! Yes! Goodbye! See you in another life!
JACKIE JACK.   *(Stepping forth.)* That's a lie! I'm his! I'm his creation!
PENDERTON.   Don't say that! They'll think you're my illegitimate son.
JACKIE JACK.   Well, I am in a way.

PENDERTON.   Stop that. You're not getting any more money out of me.
JACKIE JACK.   I'll take credit cards.
PENDERTON.   What'll you take? No! Stop! Forget it! I'm not paying you a dime.
JACKIE JACK.   You really don't want to acknowledge my existence, do you?
PENDERTON.   Well, why should I?
JACKIE JACK.   Because you created me.
PENDERTON.   I only half created you.
JACKIE JACK.   Oh. Right. You loved writing the first act.
PENDERTON.   *(Ecstatically.)* I *love* first acts.
JACKIE JACK.   But you didn't want to write the second act.
PENDERTON.   *(Depressed.)* I loathe second acts.
JACKIE JACK.   So you're like an absentee father.
PENDERTON.   What?
JACKIE JACK.   You enjoy the process of making a baby but hate the work of raising one.
PENDERTON.   What?
JACKIE JACK.   You like first acts but hate second acts.
PENDERTON.   Look, I don't have any responsibility to you. You're not my son.
JACKIE JACK.   *(Yelling to an imaginary crowd.)* Don't believe him! I'm his son! A genetic look-alike!
PENDERTON.   Would you shut up?
JACKIE JACK.   *(Screaming.)* I'm his bastard! I'm his bastard!
PENDERTON.   He is not! Wait a minute — What am I worried about? No one will believe you're my son.
JACKIE JACK.   Why not?
PENDERTON.   Well, we're about the same age, for one thing.
JACKIE JACK.   Well, of course we are — I'm your alter ego.
PENDERTON.   What?
JACKIE JACK.   I'm part of your pathetic psyche.
PENDERTON.   I resent that.
JACKIE JACK.   *You* resent that? What about me? From the very beginning your psyche was the best I had to work with. After all, I am your creation. Whatever's in act one, I know.

PENDERTON.   (*Miserably.*) Oh God.

JACKIE JACK.   Also, I read a lot.

PENDERTON.   You *read* a lot?

JACKIE JACK.   I go to libraries.

PENDERTON.   They let you in?

JACKIE JACK.   They're open to the public.

PENDERTON.   But you're a fictional character!

JACKIE JACK.   What better place for me to go. I mean, it's not like I've got a home.

PENDERTON.   Well, of course you don't have a home.

JACKIE JACK.   Well, I might have if you'd given me a second act. When we last met, if you'll recall, I was having an affair with Murray's wife. Boy was he pissed. (*Looking about.*) I hope he's not around here. Sometimes he comes out looking for me. I think he'd like to kill me. I can't be sure, of course, because certain people didn't finish the second act.

PENDERTON.   (*Frightened.*) Someone's trying to kill you? Who?

JACKIE JACK.   Murray Popkin.

PENDERTON.   Murray Popkin?

JACKIE JACK.   Sure. Murray in the first act.

PENDERTON.   There are *more* of you?

JACKIE JACK.   Of course. Everybody in the first act. In fact, all your unfinished characters are out walking around. Remember Lavonia Floogle?

PENDERTON.   (*Lovingly.*) Of course — the aspiring actress from one of my first plays —

JACKIE JACK.   A play which you never finished —

PENDERTON.   She was young, virginal —

JACKIE JACK.   Yeah, I fucked her the other night.

PENDERTON.   What?!

JACKIE JACK.   Yep. We played hide the sturgeon together the other night.

PENDERTON.   Lavonia Floogle? But she was pure, angelic!

JACKIE JACK.   Well, when you didn't finish her second act, her self-esteem went right down the toilet. She lives at the Beacon Motel. She used to be a prostitute and a heroin addict.

PENDERTON.   No!

JACKIE JACK.   But she's doing a lot better now.

PENDERTON.   Good.

JACKIE JACK.   Now, she's just a prostitute and votes Republican.

PENDERTON.   Oh, God.

JACKIE JACK.   Well, what d'you expect when you don't take responsibility for people? You can't just bring people into the world and leave them dangling.

PENDERTON.   What do you mean?

JACKIE JACK.   You didn't give Lavonia a second act. She lost hope. I mean, look around you. Half the people you see in the parks, in the subways, they ain't got no second acts, no hope.

PENDERTON.   But they're not fictional characters. They're real.

JACKIE JACK.   Oh really? Are the homeless, the bums, the alcoholics real to you? Do you see them?

PENDERTON.   Well, that's not the point.

JACKIE JACK.   It isn't? What is the point?

PENDERTON.   That fictional characters are not real. They don't just walk around.

JACKIE JACK.   Oh really? Watch out! Over there's Captain Ahab. That guy writing the poem? That's Romeo. Look, there's Huck Finn trying to pick up Cleopatra. Watch out. That guy over there? The scary one?

PENDERTON.   Who's he?

JACKIE JACK.   Maurice Gutbaum.

PENDERTON.   He *is* society.

JACKIE JACK.   He oughta be. He's a character out of a Norman Mailer novel that got rejected.

PENDERTON.   Why did he get rejected?

JACKIE JACK.   He was too psychotic. And when you're too psychotic for a Norman Mailer novel — watch out.

PENDERTON.   *(Paranoid.)* How many people around us are real and how many are not real?

JACKIE JACK.   Oh. We're all real. It's just that some of us are ghosts. Ghosts that never had a second act. Never had a chance.

PENDERTON.   No! Fictional characters don't just stroll about Central Park unattended.

JACKIE JACK.   What about Gutbaum? What about me? I'm an extension of your psyche, I'm tellin' ya.

PENDERTON.   No. No.

JACKIE JACK.   Hey, every time a poet dreams, his dreams wander off into the world to live a life of their own. Central Park is full of dreams and dreamers. Fugitives from lost poems. Raiders on reality park! Look at it, Penderton! There it is: Central Park in springtime! *Vanity Fair* on parade ... the entire panalopy of humanity wandering around with its dick in its hand. Who is to say what is real and what is not real? What has meaning and what doesn't? Which is to be saved and the other lost?

PENDERTON.   *(Caught up.)* Which one?

JACKIE JACK.   Does it matter? This is the central proposition: Whose life is worth saving? The saint? The one who lives his life for the others' common good? Or the deadbeats, the selfish ones who spend their time trying to accumulate wealth, Porsches, swimming pools, who wanna get laid by slobbering movie stars with big tits! In other words — me. Who's more important? The message or the messenger? *(Pause.)* You take Captain Ahab over there. Who's more alive — him or ol' Herman Melville? Who's more real, you or me? Think about it. Take your time.

PENDERTON.   Naaaah. You're just something I ate. Maybe that pizza I had last night.

JACKIE JACK.   Hey! I'm not just some puking piece of pepperoni, pal. I'm as real to you as anyone you've ever known.

PENDERTON.   OK. What are you?

JACKIE JACK.   Your creation.

PENDERTON.   Oh, don't start that again.

JACKIE JACK.   You created half of me.

PENDERTON.   OK, right —

JACKIE JACK.   You didn't finish the other half —

PENDERTON.   I understand —

JACKIE JACK.   In a sense, I'm half a man —

PENDERTON.   Right —

JACKIE JACK.   How would you like to be half a man?

PENDERTON.   Well, I wouldn't —

JACKIE JACK.   Well, there you go —

PENDERTON.   I know, but —

JACKIE JACK.   But nothing! Hey! Don't get me wrong! I'm perfectly functional as a man.

PENDERTON.   I'm sure you are.

JACKIE JACK.   I'm hung like a horse if you wanna know the facts.

PENDERTON.   Right.

JACKIE JACK.   They don't call me Kleisdale for nothing.

PENDERTON.   I got it.

JACKIE JACK.   Just 'cause I'm fictional doesn't mean I'm inferior. I can do what you can.

PENDERTON.   No you can't.

JACKIE JACK.   Yes I can.

PENDERTON.   Can't —

JACKIE JACK.   Can —

PENDERTON.   Can't —

JACKIE JACK.   Can —

PENDERTON.   Can't —

JACKIE JACK.   Can't —

PENDERTON.   Can —

JACKIE JACK.   Can — you see I *can* do it — *(Singing "can-can-can" from Offenbach's* Orpheus in the Underworld. *Jackie and Penderton dance.)*

PENDERTON.   Stop that! I can't be seen dancing with a non-existent human being. I'm going to be accepted into the National Academy of Arts and Letters!... one day.

JACKIE JACK.   The National Academy?! Fat chance!

PENDERTON.   And why not, may I ask?

JACKIE JACK.   Because you used to write for TV game shows, that's why!

PENDERTON.   I only did that once!

JACKIE JACK.   Once is enough to keep you out of the National Academy, pal.

PENDERTON.   Uh ... listen. I did that work under a pseud-

onym years ago and I'd just as soon keep it a secret. Here's five dollars. Keep it under your hat.
JACKIE JACK.   So — trying to get rid of me, eh?
PENDERTON.   No, no not at all!
JACKIE JACK.   You think I'm crazy, don't you?
PENDERTON.   Crazy?
JACKIE JACK.   You think I'm crazy as Gutbaum! Don't ya! Don't ya!
PENDERTON.   *(Humoring him affably.)* You know I've been waiting here all morning for something like this to happen.
JACKIE JACK.   But something like me never happens.
PENDERTON.   Well, now that it has, I can be going. To write it down. *(Penderton begins to exit.)*
JACKIE JACK.   But if you leave *now,* you'll miss the best part. *(Penderton stops, intrigued.)*
PENDERTON.   *(Suspiciously.)* What *is* the best part?
JACKIE JACK.   I don't know, but it can't have happened yet.
PENDERTON.   Why not?
JACKIE JACK.   Because then *I'll* have missed it.
PENDERTON.   Maybe that's what you've done —
JACKIE JACK.   What?
PENDERTON.   Maybe you've missed the best part of your whole life.
JACKIE JACK.   Hold on —
PENDERTON.   *(Caught up in the image.)* It's like a movie and you've walked into the middle of it.
JACKIE JACK.   I've walked into the middle of my own movie?
PENDERTON.   Exactly.
JACKIE JACK.   Well — that's what I mean — I wanna find out how I come out! I want my second act!
PENDERTON.   But that's impossible.
JACKIE JACK.   Why?
PENDERTON.   Because there *is* no second act. Nothing else happens in your movie. The projector's broken.
JACKIE JACK.   I want my money back! Management! I wanna see the management!
PENDERTON.   *(Impersonating an old creepy movie manager.)* I'm

the management.

JACKIE JACK.   Well, management, I wanna watch more of me.

PENDERTON.   There is no more of you. I suggest you sit down, enjoy your popcorn and watch the cartoons.

JACKIE JACK.   The cartoons.

PENDERTON.   The cartoons.

JACKIE JACK.   But I wanna watch my life.

PENDERTON.   The cartoons would do just as well.

JACKIE JACK.   Are the cartoons good?

PENDERTON.   Most people like them.

JACKIE JACK.   Are they as good as the picture?

PENDERTON.   Most people can't tell the difference.

JACKIE JACK.   Are the cartoons funny, at least?

PENDERTON.   The cartoons are hilarious except when they're hideous.

JACKIE JACK.   I like a cartoon with a good laugh.

PENDERTON.   We've got those. They're called "Other People's Cartoons." Sit down.

JACKIE JACK.   Are they funny?

PENDERTON.   Hilarious.

JACKIE JACK.   I wanna see the most hilarious cartoon you've got.

PENDERTON.   No problem. Sit down.

JACKIE JACK.   This one's hilarious, right?

PENDERTON.   Hilarious.

JACKIE JACK.   I'll laugh?

PENDERTON.   You'll shit a brick.

JACKIE JACK.   What's it about?

PENDERTON.   "Your Sex Life."

JACKIE JACK.   "My Sex Life."

PENDERTON.   That's right.

JACKIE JACK.   And it's funny?

PENDERTON.   Hilarious. People can't get enough of it. Sit down.

JACKIE JACK.   And it's about my sex life.

PENDERTON.   What there was of it …

JACKIE JACK.   Chuck …

PENDERTON.   What, Jackie?

JACKIE JACK.   Will you do me a favor?

PENDERTON.   What?

JACKIE JACK.   Will you watch the cartoon of my sex life with me?

PENDERTON.   Well, of course I will.

JACKIE JACK.   Would you hold my hand?

PENDERTON.   Of course. *(They sit.)*

JACKIE JACK.   Ever since I was a kid, I've been really scared of cartoons.

PENDERTON.   Why?

JACKIE JACK.   I'm afraid they might be me. *(Anxiety.)* Where's my popcorn? Where's my Nehi orange? Where's my Moon Pie? Where's my 3 Musketeers bar? Where's my Malted Milk Balls? I can't watch a cartoon of my sex life without my Malted Milk Balls.

PENDERTON.   Think about it. Would it make it any better?

JACKIE JACK.   At least lemme have some popcorn.

PENDERTON.   Popcorn? Of course. *(Penderton mimes handing Jackie Jack a box of popcorn. Penderton takes one for himself. Jackie Jack mimes putting some "salt" on the popcorn and hands the "salt" to Penderton. Penderton adds "salt" as he watches Jack begin to eat the non-existent popcorn. As Jackie Jack chews the popcorn, there is an enormously loud <u>sound effect</u> of the popcorn being chewed, followed by the "Clicka-Clicka-Clicka" effect of an old film projector. The lights are dimmed somewhat. They both hum along to music such as the "Merry Melody."* They then fall silent as they watch the cartoon. We watch their expressions of horror and hilarity as they react in silence to what is happening on the "screen." They have opposite, simultaneous reactions to what they see. Their emotions run the gamut from fear, titillation, humor, hope, boredom, angst, horror to despair. At the end of the film, they both hum the last of music such as the "Merry Melody"* theme. Penderton is profoundly disturbed. Is he hallucinating?)*

JACKIE JACK.   *(Chipper.)* So that was your sex life?

PENDERTON.   I thought it was yours —

* See Special Note on Songs and Recordings on copyright page.

JACKIE JACK.   Well, what's yours is mine —
PENDERTON.   That was horrible.
JACKIE JACK.   I dunno. When you were young, your life had a *"Je ne sais quoi"* quality to it.
PENDERTON.   Is that what that was?
JACKIE JACK.   Of course, when you got old, it was more *"corpus delicti." (Penderton panics. Rises to leave.)* Stop! Where are you going?
PENDERTON.   I'm leaving.
JACKIE JACK.   Why?
PENDERTON.   I've got an appointment.
JACKIE JACK.   No, you don't.
PENDERTON.   I'm expected.
JACKIE JACK.   No, you aren't.
PENDERTON.   I'm, uh, I'm — hungry.
JACKIE JACK.   No, you're not.
PENDERTON.   You know ... you're right ... I don't know where I'm going.
JACKIE JACK.   So what's all the fuss about? Stay and write me a second act.
PENDERTON.   Forget it. I've told you. You're a failed character. You're not funny and you're not tragic — get a life.
JACKIE JACK.   That's what I'm trying to do.
PENDERTON.   Look, I'm a busy man! I've got things to do. I've got to get to work.
JACKIE JACK.   You're *not* going to work.
PENDERTON.   What? I, well, I most certainly am!
JACKIE JACK.   No, you're not.
PENDERTON.   I've been here thinking all morning — preparing to write.
JACKIE JACK.   You haven't been thinking, you've been procrastinating.
PENDERTON.   Procrastinating?! Me?!
JACKIE JACK.   You've been procrastinating for months. Years.
PENDERTON.   What?!
JACKIE JACK.   You haven't had an original idea in centuries. All you do is play it safe! Writing what's expected of you —

PENDERTON.   No! No! I'm obsessed! That's it! I'm a writer that's obsessed with a theme!

JACKIE JACK.   What's your theme? Procrastination?

PENDERTON.   That was my *old* theme.

JACKIE JACK.   Your old theme?

PENDERTON.   It was a great theme! Twentieth century man is confronted by a myriad of dire disasters. War! Plague! Famine! And what does man do? He procrastinates! I was going to write the definitive play about procrastination!

JACKIE JACK.   What happened?

PENDERTON.   I never got around to it.

JACKIE JACK.   See there! All talk, no action!

PENDERTON.   I'm leaving. *(He doesn't move.)*

JACKIE JACK.   See there, you can't even take a step.

PENDERTON.   *(Despairing.)* Why, once I could write for hours on end ... sometimes even completing ... entire sentences.

JACKIE JACK.   Now all you do is plagiarize.

PENDERTON.   I don't plagiarize ... I don't plagiarize ... I pay homage.

JACKIE JACK.   Homage! Ha! You'd strip the bones off dead poets like a Turk.

PENDERTON.   It's true! My talent is gone!

JACKIE JACK.   Gone!

PENDERTON.   Finished —

JACKIE JACK.   Finished —

PENDERTON.   Kaput —

JACKIE JACK.   Kaput —

PENDERTON.   Farewell —

JACKIE JACK.   Farewell —

PENDERTON.   Dead!

JACKIE JACK.   Dead!

PENDERTON.   I can't stand it! *(Penderton breaks down, weeps on Jackie Jack's shoulder.)*

JACKIE JACK.   There, there —

PENDERTON.   *(Renewed angst.)* "Farewell, Farewell! The tranquil mind! Farewell content!"

JACKIE JACK.   There, there —

PENDERTON.   "Farewell the plumed troops!"

JACKIE JACK.   Goodbye the troops —
PENDERTON.   "Farewell the neighing steed —"
JACKIE JACK.   RRRRRH! *(Jack "neighs" and "rears" like a horse.)*
PENDERTON.   "Farewell! The immortal Jove's dead! Farewell! Othello's occupation's gone!" *(Penderton collapses. Jackie Jack consoles him. Tragically.)* So, you see — there's nothing else for me to do but ... to ... to ... to —
JACKIE JACK.   No, not that.
PENDERTON.   Yes.
JACKIE JACK.   Anything but that —
PENDERTON.   Yes! I've got to sell out the National Academy of Arts and Letters.
JACKIE JACK.   But that'll mean —
PENDERTON.   Yes, acceptance! Wealth! Fame! Immortality!
JACKIE JACK.   You're not going to sell out for a cheap gimmick like immortality, are you?
PENDERTON.   *(Sickened.)* Why not.
JACKIE JACK.   You'll have to give them what they want —
PENDERTON.   What they expect.
JACKIE JACK.   What they want!
PENDERTON.   All the cheap jokes —
JACKIE JACK.   All the cheap gags —
PENDERTON.   I'll have to crank out all the usual shit —
JACKIE JACK.   You'll crank it out?
PENDERTON.   I'll crank it out.
JACKIE JACK.   Even the profound shit?
PENDERTON.   Even the profound shit.
JACKIE JACK.   Where will you keep getting it? All of this shit?
PENDERTON.   I'll go back to my roots. To my childhood. To my guts.
JACKIE JACK.   You'll plagiarize?
PENDERTON.   *(Smugly.)* There's always *Finnegan's Wake*. No one's read that one.
JACKIE JACK.   Please. Won't you help me?
PENDERTON.   What d'you want from me?
JACKIE JACK.   Just a second act! Is that too much to ask?

PENDERTON.   What do you want a second act for?

JACKIE JACK.   I'm so lonely.

PENDERTON.   Lonely? You've gotta be kidding. You get to make it with other fictional characters. Go find some Carson McCullers reject. Quit bothering me.

JACKIE JACK.   Oh, if that's all I wanted that would be easy. I mean, I can make it with Goldie Hawn and Julie Christie anytime I want.

PENDERTON.   What?

JACKIE JACK.   Yeah. Goldie Hawn and Julie Christie in an early draft of the movie *Shampoo.* They have this sex scene together with Warren Beatty. It was written but then rejected because it was just too sexy. Now their characters are wandering around through eternity hornier then hell, looking for Mr. Right.

PENDERTON.   Goldie Hawn and Julie Christie. What year?

JACKIE JACK.   1974.

PENDERTON.   My God! A threesome with Goldie Hawn and Julie Christie 1974! That's career prime!

JACKIE JACK.   But you don't understand. That's someone else's second act. I want my own second act.

PENDERTON.   Forget it. It's too much work. You said yourself all I do is procrastinate and plagiarize.

JACKIE JACK.   But you created me! You're like my god. I'm like your little sonny boy. Don't you want your little sonny boy to be happy?

PENDERTON.   No.

JACKIE JACK.   Why not?

PENDERTON.   I'm your god and I'm not happy.

JACKIE JACK.   So if you're not happy, none of your creatures get to be happy?

PENDERTON.   That's it.

JACKIE JACK.   I can't believe it. My god is a vindictive god.

PENDERTON.   Look. I couldn't write your second act — I didn't know how.

JACKIE JACK.   Well — this is a chance to redeem yourself!

PENDERTON.   It's too late.

JACKIE JACK.   I just want something that's real, that's true,

that's fully felt!
PENDERTON.   At these prices, you want "fully felt?"
JACKIE JACK.   Look, I don't even care if my second act is tragic or even mediocre, as long as it's mine!
PENDERTON.   (*Evasively.*) Well, look, maybe I can crank something out over the weekend —
JACKIE JACK.   No! It can't be some glib piece of commercial crap hiding behind a cynical facade.
PENDERTON.   But that's what I do best!
JACKIE JACK.   That's what you've done for twenty years.
PENDERTON.   It's what I do.
JACKIE JACK.   It's what you know.
PENDERTON.   It's so I won't think.
JACKIE JACK.   It's so you won't feel.
PENDERTON.   It's why I get up.
JACKIE JACK.   You can still get up?
PENDERTON.   Not often.
JACKIE JACK.   Some mornings —
PENDERTON.   Are like some nights.
JACKIE JACK.   They're like one and the same.
PENDERTON.   Oh God! If only I'd gone into television sooner, I'd have residuals by now.
JACKIE JACK.   Now's the time for a total break with everything you've ever written!
PENDERTON.   No! The risks are too great.
JACKIE JACK.   Risks? What risks?
PENDERTON.   The risk of ruining my reputation.
JACKIE JACK.   What reputation?
PENDERTON.   The greatest reputation an artist can have: obscurity.
JACKIE JACK.   (*Loud.*) Give me vaudeville!
PENDERTON.   If I muck it up at this point, they may figure out what a fraud I was all along.
JACKIE JACK.   "There was a young girl from Nantuckett —"
PENDERTON.   I've never finished anything: genius is denial.
JACKIE JACK.   But your other plays had endings.
PENDERTON.   Pah! Sentimental bilge!
JACKIE JACK.   You're in a rut!

PENDERTON.   I'm in a rut!

JACKIE JACK.   Astound your critics.

PENDERTON.   Who needs 'em?

JACKIE JACK.   Horrify your public.

PENDERTON.   Who needs 'em!

JACKIE JACK.   Scandalize the Academy!

PENDERTON.   Now, wait a minute. There's nothing I wouldn't do to get into the Academy.

JACKIE JACK.   Well, you won't get in until you write me a second act ... *give me a second act.*

PENDERTON.   You're right. No more excuses! No more procrastination! I have a story to tell and I must tell it! True, there are others who could, if called upon, tell the tale better than I. But here, at this juncture in time, I am the only story teller. The only artist to tell this tale of "Jackie Jack, the Sturgeon King." Even if the tale is not worth telling. Even if no one is here to hear it. I must tell this tale of one man's struggling against sex, death and the meaning of existence! Say — this is a much bigger project than I expected! I wonder if I'm up to it?

JACKIE JACK.   I have faith in you.

PENDERTON.   Really?

JACKIE JACK.   Hell no.

PENDERTON.   To begin with — where was I?

JACKIE JACK.   The end of the first act.

PENDERTON.   All right! First thing we need is a plot. What have we got?

JACKIE JACK.   Well, when last we left me, I was having an affair with Murray Popkin's wife.

PENDERTON.   Boy meets girl. I like it.

JACKIE JACK.   She's not a girl, she's an old bag.

PENDERTON.   An old bag? OK, it's a new wrinkle on an old theme.

JACKIE JACK.   Wrinkles? She was old enough to be my mother.

PENDERTON.   *(Considering it.)* What if she *were* your mother?... Nah. It's been done. That Sophocles. What a pig for plots.

JACKIE JACK.   I made love to her once in a cemetery.
PENDERTON.   Did she enjoy it?
JACKIE JACK.   She didn't know whether she was coming or going.
PENDERTON.   But why, Jackie, why, did you desire Murray Popkin's wife? *Pour quois* Popkin?
JACKIE JACK.   Well, she was over six feet tall.
PENDERTON.   You climbed her because she was there! Like the Matterhorn!
JACKIE JACK.   Right. I was so horny it didn't matter. *(Silence. They sense the audience's hostility.)* They're getting hostile.
PENDERTON.   What do they expect at these prices?
JACKIE JACK.   Better go into our dance.
PENDERTON.   I'll try a joke —
JACKIE JACK.   The jokes are why we're going into the dance.
PENDERTON.   What'll they do if we don't?
JACKIE JACK.   They'll stone us.
PENDERTON.   What do we call this dance?
JACKIE JACK.   The Ghost Dance. *(They do a little dance step. They hum Strauss's "Blue Danube Waltz" for a few bars. Penderton is now sweating bullets.)*
PENDERTON.   Now then, how did you seduce Mrs. Popkin?
JACKIE JACK.   I hit her in the face with a sturgeon.
PENDERTON.   That's what I mean. I can't write a second act to that.
JACKIE JACK.   Why not?
PENDERTON.   It has no tragic dimension.
JACKIE JACK.   I could slap her in the face with a flounder.
PENDERTON.   No. *(Realizing.)* ... it's no good ...
JACKIE JACK.   How 'bout a nice big halibut steak?
PENDERTON.   It still wouldn't be tragic.
JACKIE JACK.   Could it be comic?
PENDERTON.   *(Dejected.)* I suppose if it was funny.
JACKIE JACK.   What if I threw a handful of scungilli in her face?
PENDERTON.   I don't think so. *(Kindly.)* You see, Jackie, as I remember it, your character — in the first act does a lotta

things ...
JACKIE JACK.   Hey! I've got a big part in act one.
PENDERTON.   *(Realizing it all.)* A lot of things ... a lotta things.
JACKIE JACK.   In act one, I'm a star. It's just that in act two — because of it's non-existent nature — my part kinda tapers off.
PENDERTON.   No. See, in the first act, you lie and steal and cheat. You ruin people's lives. You're a mean, vicious drunk. A horrible person. A loathsome, despicable character.
JACKIE JACK.   At least I've got a big part.
PENDERTON.   And at the end, remember ... remember ...
JACKIE JACK.   Sure. My wife leaves me, I have a nervous breakdown and try to kill myself. It's a terrific scene. And then I end up on a park bench alone, talking to myself, crazy as a loon. *(Pause. Jackie Jack goes to his bag. Penderton stares out.)*
PENDERTON.   What're you doing?
JACKIE JACK.   Gettin' my bag.
PENDERTON.   Why?
JACKIE JACK.   We can't stay here.
PENDERTON.   We can't? It's a public park.
JACKIE JACK.   They'll douse us with gasoline and set us on fire.
PENDERTON.   Who will?
JACKIE JACK.   Kids. Everybody.
PENDERTON.   I'm staying.
JACKIE JACK.   You can't stay here. It's getting dark. *(Pause.)*
PENDERTON.   How long were we here?
JACKIE JACK.   I dunno.
PENDERTON.   Were we here yesterday?
JACKIE JACK.   I dunno. C'mon, we gotta go.
PENDERTON.   We do?
JACKIE JACK.   Everybody else has gone.
PENDERTON.   Who?
JACKIE JACK.   Oh. Gutbaum. Captain Ahab. Romeo.
PENDERTON.   Gone, huh?
JACKIE JACK.   Gone with the wind.
PENDERTON.   There is no wind. *(They begin to walk off.)*

Well, you don't seem to be taking this so badly.
JACKIE JACK.   Well, I'm not the one who's lost his mind.
PENDERTON.   Do we come here everyday?
JACKIE JACK.   Every day.
PENDERTON.   What do we do?
JACKIE JACK.   We work on the second act.
PENDERTON.   Do I ever get into the Academy?
JACKIE JACK.   Who knows? But I mean, do you care?
PENDERTON.   Hell, no! To hell with Academy! To hell with everyone!
JACKIE JACK.   Then there's Lavonia Floogle.
PENDERTON.   My actress! My ideal! My virginal actress!
JACKIE JACK.   Hey, two out of three.
PENDERTON.   Is she real?
JACKIE JACK.   To you? Very real. *(They walk. Stop.)* One thing.
PENDERTON.   What?
JACKIE JACK.   I snore.

FADE

PROPERTY LIST

New York Times newspaper (PENDERTON)
Huge cigar (JACKIE JACK)
Bag (JACKIE JACK) with:
        napkin
        half-eaten sandwich
Half-pint bottle of whiskey (JACKIE JACK)
Bunch of tulips (JACKIE JACK)
Sturgeon   (JACKIE JACK)
Wallet (PENDERTON)
Money (bills) (PENDERTON)

SOUND EFFECTS

Crunching sound of popcorn being chewed
"Clicka-clicka-clicka" of old film projector

NEW
PLAYS

THE AFRICAN COMPANY PRESENTS
RICHARD III
by Carlyle Brown

EDWARD ALBEE'S
FRAGMENTS and THE MARRIAGE PLAY

IMAGINARY LIFE
by Peter Parnell

MIXED EMOTIONS
by Richard Baer

THE SWAN
by Elizabeth Egloff

Write for information as to
availability
DRAMATISTS PLAY SERVICE, Inc.
440 Park Avenue South   New York, N.Y. 10016

NEW
PLAYS

THE LIGHTS
by Howard Korder

THE TRIUMPH OF LOVE
by James Magruder

LATER LIFE
by A.R. Gurney

THE LOMAN FAMILY PICNIC
by Donald Margulies

A PERFECT GANESH
by Terrence McNally

SPAIN
by Romulus Linney

Write for information as to availability

DRAMATISTS PLAY SERVICE, Inc.

440 Park Avenue South　　　New York, N.Y. 10016

NEW
PLAYS

LONELY PLANET
by Steven Dietz

THE AMERICA PLAY
by Suzan-Lori Parks

THE FOURTH WALL
by A.R. Gurney

JULIE JOHNSON
by Wendy Hammond

FOUR DOGS AND A BONE
by John Patrick Shanley

DESDEMONA, A PLAY ABOUT A
HANDKERCHIEF
by Paula Vogel

Write for information as to
availability
DRAMATISTS PLAY SERVICE, Inc.
440 Park Avenue South   New York, N.Y. 10016